Midge is a toad
a wonderful toad, is she, you see

and these words come from me, and I
found little Midge

under a bush near a tree, and there she was
on that perfect day, in that place,

looking up at my face,

Oh Midge, what a toad
you are

You are a star

so timid and shy
waiting and watching a bug going by

I'd like, I think, to take you home, oh yes,
but I know,

you'll be happier here, with the trees and green grass
near other toads who come by your way

and frogs, too, may want to share,
or may want to play

in a toad way, of course, near the rocks or a stream
and sleep near the pebbles and dream a toad dream

so its time to go home now, for me, that is, and you,
dear Midge,
can hop to the stream

My lunch is waiting
I'm having cream cheese and jelly

Oh Midge,
I can see, you have quite a large belly

Perhaps you and your frog friend too,
are hungry for lunch
or ice cream or even a drink
oh my, did I think

you might share my sandwich
or a potato chip

or even from my drink, take a toad type sip,
but no, you have your own idea of a delicious meal,

a worm, an ant
a stem from a plant

a sip of water from a nearby puddle
is where, with others, you like to huddle

and then, perhaps, a bath in the mud
or an hour beneath the blue sky

no, you would not like to share,
my french fry

and you like to hop
not sip my soda pop

so Midge, I am saying goodbye, to you, and I'm hoping
your toad wishes, all come happily true, from your
friend for an hour, xx
Mary Sue.

Toads have many frog friends

Here are some interesting facts about toads

Toad babies are called tadpoles.

They are born in the water,

usually in a pond or stream, sometimes even in a large puddle.

They absorb their tail, and become toads!

Toads do not drink water from their mouths.

Instead, they lie in water, and absorb the water into their skin.

they search for bugs with their eyes

and will only eat a bug or worm if it is moving.

Toads change color according to what they are lying on.

If they are in the woods, they will become more brown in color, and if they are on grass, they will change color to be almost green in color.

Toads hibernate for the winter

They do not cause warts

Toads like to sleep under logs

They like shady areas and rocks

Large toads can eat up to four bugs per day

Small toads can eat up to two bugs per day

Toads live in gardens and can live in a little house of their own!

www.ingramcontent.com/pod-product-compliance
Lightning Source LLC
Chambersburg PA
CBHW050856290526
45792CB00002B/614